Gentlemen might be in short supply today, but this little book of wisdom could be a cure. If you're a young man who cares about the quality of his mark on the world—or if you know such a young man—the aphorisms of *The Gentleman's Handbook* may prove a helpful guide.

The Gentleman's Handbook

A Guide to Exemplary Behavior
OR
Rules of Life and Love for
Men Who Care

Aaron Shepard

Shepard Publications
Friday Harbor, Washington

Version 1.2

Contents

GENTLEMEN

A Gentleman in Love

A GENTLEMAN always finds a compliment for a lady he loves.

A GENTLEMAN compliments a lady not to gain anything from her but to give her pleasure.

A GENTLEMAN puts a lady's pleasure before his own.

A GENTLEMAN overcomes his own fear to save a lady from suffering hers.

A GENTLEMAN welcomes being told by a lady what will please her.

A GENTLEMAN discovers a lady's tastes instead of imposing his own.

A GENTLEMAN observes how a lady treats him to understand how she wants to be treated.

A GENTLEMAN is always happy to extend small courtesies to a lady but will not persist if they are unwelcome.

A GENTLEMAN returns a toilet seat to where a lady will expect to find it.

A GENTLEMAN does not attempt to buy love, nor does he expect to receive it and give nothing in return.

A GENTLEMAN may let a lady know what pleases him, but does not let her feel obligated to provide it.

A GENTLEMAN may be grateful to a lady for household help but must never expect it.

A GENTLEMAN allows a lady to enlarge his interests, not merely support them.

A GENTLEMAN never leaves a lady guessing.

A GENTLEMAN lets a lady know she's wanted, then waits for her to reveal the same.

A GENTLEMAN never causes a lady to feel unlovely, even when he must decline her favors.

A GENTLEMAN accepts a lady's no, even when he does not believe it.

A GENTLEMAN honors the limits set by a lady, even when she wishes to forget them herself.

A GENTLEMAN never accepts from a lady what he believes she will regret giving.

A GENTLEMAN never speaks to others of a lady's favors.

A GENTLEMAN never compares one lady to another.

A GENTLEMAN is faithful even when faithfulness is not returned.

A GENTLEMAN never stops caring for one he has loved.

A GENTLEMAN never denies the truth of his love, even when it's past.

A GENTLEMAN always feels privileged by a lady's company.

A GENTLEMAN does not ask a lady to be other than she is.

A GENTLEMAN gives a lady everything he can without compromising himself.

A GENTLEMAN remains a gentleman, even if a lady seeks the opposite.

A GENTLEMAN knows that a lady may not always want a gentleman in bed.

A GENTLEMAN knows that a lady's greatest gift is herself.

A GENTLEMAN understands that every lady is a flower, and that love will make her bloom.

GENTLEMEN

A Gentleman in Speech

A GENTLEMAN listens carefully to others and takes pains to remember what he hears.

A GENTLEMAN listens till the end, even if he knows what will be said.

A GENTLEMAN knows that what is said is often just a shield for what is felt.

A GENTLEMAN accepts an excuse even when clearly false.

A GENTLEMAN invites confidences but respects privacy.

A GENTLEMAN knows that the secret shared by another must stop with him.

A GENTLEMAN knows that to tell a secret to one person is to tell it to the world.

A GENTLEMAN addresses others as they wish to be addressed.

A GENTLEMAN considers the effect of his words before he speaks.

A GENTLEMAN speaks carefully to avoid being misunderstood.

A GENTLEMAN observes the reactions of others to see if his words are received as intended.

A GENTLEMAN aims to speak only what is kind, true, and helpful.

A GENTLEMAN will never lie to gain advantage, but may depart from truth to avoid giving pain.

A GENTLEMAN may accept blame to end conflict, even if it does not belong to him.

A GENTLEMAN may display his temper,
but will never let it loose.

A GENTLEMAN avoids language that shocks in any way not needed.

A GENTLEMAN does not need to be in the right.

A GENTLEMAN offers knowledge and wisdom to others without insisting they relinquish error.

A GENTLEMAN never smirks.

A GENTLEMAN surrenders the last word.

A GENTLEMAN withholds a parting sting even when one is in hand.

A GENTLEMAN knows that the best way to handle an insult is to deflect it.

A GENTLEMAN does not condemn, so as to leave others room to grow.

A GENTLEMAN knows that words should be weighed, not counted.

GENTLEMEN

A Gentleman in Society

A GENTLEMAN understands that the value of any person goes far beyond their usefulness to him.

A GENTLEMAN does not take chances with the well-being of others.

A GENTLEMAN holds that inflicting pain or suffering is never an option.

A GENTLEMAN never cares if the good he gives will come back.

A GENTLEMAN encourages the best in everyone, though requiring perfection only in himself.

A GENTLEMAN accepts the weaknesses of others without allowing those weaknesses in himself.

A GENTLEMAN never looks down on others less capable.

A GENTLEMAN allows others to make their own mistakes.

A GENTLEMAN does not try to change the actions of others when he can instead simply prevent them.

A GENTLEMAN never blames others for his own behavior.

A GENTLEMAN believes that everyone means well, however they may fail at it.

A GENTLEMAN honors another's dedication to principles even when they conflict with his own.

A GENTLEMAN always chooses compassion over righteousness.

A GENTLEMAN never restricts his loyalty to those like himself.

A GENTLEMAN does not let others dictate his loyalties.

A GENTLEMAN does not let others decide for him what is right or wrong.

A GENTLEMAN never takes orders to do what he would not feel right to do on his own.

A GENTLEMAN honors his competitors and may help them when they stumble.

A GENTLEMAN strives to be first but can accept being last.

A GENTLEMAN neither seeks nor accepts unfair advantage.

A GENTLEMAN does not seek profit from the hardship of others.

A GENTLEMAN takes no delight in the misfortune of opponents.

A GENTLEMAN knows that the best way to disarm opponents is often to befriend them.

A GENTLEMAN befriends those around him to ease disputes that may later arise.

A GENTLEMAN knows that attacks are often best handled by stepping out of their way to let them pass.

A GENTLEMAN knows that to respond to attacks is to give them strength.

A GENTLEMAN knows that, in any dispute, two winners is better than one.

A GENTLEMAN knows that most unpleasantness received from others has nothing to do with him at all.

A GENTLEMAN delights in children and honors the elderly.

A GENTLEMAN never tells a child how to grow up.

A GENTLEMAN does not expect his children to be himself.

A GENTLEMAN forgives his parents for not being more perfect than he is.

A GENTLEMAN does not foul the air, minds, or lives of others.

A GENTLEMAN does not leave messes for others to clean up.

A GENTLEMAN knows how to do his own laundry.

A GENTLEMAN never cloaks in anonymity what would shame him if revealed.

A GENTLEMAN avoids ugliness in clothes or styling, even if it's the fashion.

A GENTLEMAN does not ignore those beside him to address those who are distant.

A GENTLEMAN is on time, so as to not make others wait.

A GENTLEMAN remembers birthdays and other special days, even if he has to set reminders.

A GENTLEMAN knows that a smile costs nothing and may mean the world to one who receives it.

A GENTLEMAN knows that his smile means nothing if not backed by concern.

A GENTLEMAN knows that a gift means most to the one who gives it.

A GENTLEMAN knows that the greatest gift is to receive a gift graciously.

A GENTLEMAN may accept help just for the sake of the helper.

A GENTLEMAN knows that money with strings comes at too high a price.

A GENTLEMAN loans only what he can do without.

A GENTLEMAN does not promise more than he can deliver.

A GENTLEMAN makes no commitment he cannot keep.

A GENTLEMAN does not leave when he is needed or stay when he can do no good.

A GENTLEMAN knows he cannot help others if he does not stand on firm ground himself.

GENTLEMEN

A Gentleman in Life

A GENTLEMAN knows that what he does is less important than how he does it.

A GENTLEMAN answers first to himself.

A GENTLEMAN may be obedient by choice, but declines to see obedience as either duty or virtue.

A GENTLEMAN places principle above profit.

A GENTLEMAN sets his ideals beyond his behavior.

A GENTLEMAN never lowers his standards to meet his behavior.

A GENTLEMAN does not measure his strength by the weakness of others.

A GENTLEMAN always tries to improve himself, even when no one else cares.

A GENTLEMAN forgives his own lapses, but never excuses them and resolves to do better.

A GENTLEMAN knows there is always more to the truth than he can see.

A GENTLEMAN is never too proud to accept another's greater knowledge.

A GENTLEMAN knows he may learn from anyone, even those who know less than he.

A GENTLEMAN is never afraid to be proven wrong, if it means learning what is right.

A GENTLEMAN acknowledges his own mistakes, because he knows there is no other way to grow past them.

A GENTLEMAN does not avoid what should be resolved.

A GENTLEMAN tries to address a problem at its root so it does not recur.

A GENTLEMAN is ready to give up what no longer serves him or others.

A GENTLEMAN knows that nothing is accomplished without making a choice.

A GENTLEMAN resists starting more than he can finish.

A GENTLEMAN allows for the unexpected.

A GENTLEMAN leaves time to refresh his spirit.

A GENTLEMAN does not consider it weakness to laugh at himself.

A GENTLEMAN knows that tears are not shameful if sincere.

A GENTLEMAN knows there is no virtue in either youth or old age, and no shame in them, either.

A GENTLEMAN knows that life owes him nothing, and expects to earn what he gets.

A GENTLEMAN knows there are few things he cannot do without.

A GENTLEMAN knows that the cost of possession is not limited to the cost of acquisition.

A GENTLEMAN does not take more than he can carry.

A GENTLEMAN avoids spending more than he has.

A GENTLEMAN does not spend to his limit but holds something in reserve.

A gentlemen expects a rise in expenses and allows for a lessening of income.

A GENTLEMAN gambles only with what he can afford to lose.

A GENTLEMAN pays his debts to others before himself.

A GENTLEMAN does not practice unhealthful habits or encourage others to do so.

A GENTLEMAN remains sober so he can control his actions.

A GENTLEMAN does not tempt himself with influences he thinks he can control.

A GENTLEMAN avoids doing what he must conceal.

A GENTLEMAN knows that happiness is one part seeking what he desires and two parts appreciating what he is given.

A GENTLEMAN knows that his worth is measured not by what he collects but by what he contributes.

Aaron Shepard is an author, photographer, publisher, and aspiring gentleman. He lives with his wife and fellow author, Anne L. Watson, in Friday Harbor, Washington.

Also of interest . . .

LIVING APART TOGETHER

A Unique Path to Marital Happiness

OR

The Joy of Sharing Lives Without Sharing an Address

Anne L. Watson

CPSIA information can be obtained
at www.ICGtesting.com
Printed in the USA
LVHW111158301218
601759LV00014B/39/P

9 781620 355084